Charter for the Protection of Children and Young People

ALSO INCLUDES

Essential Norms for Diocesan/Eparchial Policies Dealing with Allegations of Sexual Abuse of Minors by Priests or Deacons

A Statement of Episcopal Commitment

REVISED JUNE 2018

UNITED STATES CONFERENCE OF CATHOLIC BISHOPS

The revised *Charter for the Protection of Children and Young People* was developed by the Ad Hoc Committee for Sexual Abuse of the United States Conference of Catholic Bishops (USCCB). It was approved by the full body of U.S. Catholic bishops at its June 2005 Plenary Assembly, and this third revision was approved at the June 2018 Plenary Assembly. The revised *Essential Norms for Diocesan/Eparchial Policies Dealing with Allegations of Sexual Abuse of Minors by Priests or Deacons* was developed by the Ad Hoc Committee on Sexual Abuse of the USCCB and by the Vatican-U.S. Bishops' Mixed Commission on Sex Abuse Norms. They were approved by the full body of bishops at its June 2005 General Meeting, received the subsequent *recognitio* of the Holy See on January 1, 2006, and were promulgated May 5, 2006. The revised *Statement of Episcopal Commitment* was developed by the Ad Hoc Committee on Bishops' Life and Ministry of the USCCB. It was approved by the full body of U.S. Catholic bishops at its November 2005 Plenary Assembly and then again in 2011 and 2018. This revised edition, containing all three documents, is authorized for publication by the undersigned.

Msgr. J. Brian Bransfield
General Secretary, USCCB

Scripture texts used in this work are taken from the *New American Bible*, copyright © 1991, 1986, and 1970 by the Confraternity of Christian Doctrine, Washington, DC 20017 and are used by permission of the copyright owner. All rights reserved.

Revised edition, first printing, July 2018
Second printing, September 2018

ISBN 978-1-60137-597-1

Copyright © 2002, 2011, 2018, United States Conference of Catholic Bishops, Washington, DC. All rights reserved.

✝ CONTENTS

Charter for the Protection of Children and Young People 1
    Preamble 3
    To Promote Healing and Reconciliation with
        Victims/Survivors of Sexual Abuse of Minors 10
    To Guarantee an Effective Response to Allegations of
        Sexual Abuse of Minors 12
    To Ensure the Accountability of Our Procedures 15
    To Protect the Faithful in the Future 18
    Conclusion... 21

Essential Norms for Diocesan/Eparchial Policies
Dealing with Allegations of Sexual Abuse of
Minors by Priests or Deacons 25
    Decree of Promulgation 26
    Preamble.. 27
    Norms 29

A Statement of Episcopal Commitment 37

Charter for the Protection of Children and Young People

✝ PREAMBLE

Since 2002, the Church in the United States has experienced a crisis without precedent in our times. The sexual abuse[1] of children and young people by some deacons, priests, and bishops, and the ways in which these crimes and sins were addressed, have caused enormous pain, anger, and confusion for victims, their families, and the entire Church. As bishops, we have acknowledged our mistakes and our roles in that suffering, and we apologize and take responsibility again for too often failing victims and the Catholic people in the past. From the depths of our hearts, we bishops express great sorrow and profound regret for what the Catholic people have endured.

We share Pope Francis' "conviction that everything possible must be done to rid the Church of the scourge of the sexual abuse of minors and to open pathways of reconciliation and healing for those who were abused" (Letter of His Holiness Pope Francis to the Presidents of the Episcopal Conferences and Superiors of Institutes of Consecrated Life and Societies of Apostolic Life Concerning the Pontifical Commission for the Protection of Minors, February 2, 2015).

Again, with this 2018 revision of the *Charter for the Protection of Children and Young People*, we re-affirm our deep commitment to sustain and strengthen a safe environment within the Church for children and youth. We have listened to the profound pain and suffering of those victimized by sexual abuse and will continue to respond to their cries. We have agonized over the sinfulness, the criminality, and the breach of trust perpetrated by some members of the clergy. We have determined as best we can the extent of the problem of this abuse of minors by clergy in our country, as well as its causes and context. We will use what we have learned to strengthen the protection given to the children and young people in our care.

We continue to have a special care for and a commitment to reaching out to the victims of sexual abuse and their families. The damage caused by sexual abuse of minors is devastating and long-lasting. We apologize to each victim for the grave harm that has been inflicted on him or her, and we offer our help now and for the future. The loss of trust that is often the consequence of such abuse becomes even more tragic when it leads to a loss of the faith that we have a sacred duty to foster. We make our own the words of St. John Paul II: that the sexual abuse of young people is "by every standard wrong and rightly considered a crime by society; it is also an appalling sin in the eyes of God" (Address to the Cardinals of the United States and Conference Officers, April 23, 2002). We will continue to help victims recover from these crimes and strive to prevent these tragedies from occurring.

Along with the victims and their families, the entire Catholic community in this country has suffered because of this scandal and its consequences. The intense public scrutiny of the minority of the ordained who have betrayed their calling has caused the vast majority of faithful priests and deacons to experience enormous vulnerability to being misunderstood in their ministry and often casts over them an undeserved air of suspicion. We share with all priests and deacons a firm commitment to renewing the integrity of the vocation to Holy Orders so that it will continue to be perceived as a life of service to others after the example of Christ our Lord.

We, who have been given the responsibility of shepherding God's people, will, with his help and in full collaboration with all the faithful, continue to work to restore the bonds of trust that unite us. We have seen that words alone cannot accomplish this goal. We will continue to take action in our Plenary Assembly and at home in our dioceses and eparchies.

We feel a particular responsibility for "the ministry of reconciliation" (2 Cor 5:18) which God, who reconciled us to himself through Christ, has given us. The love of Christ impels us to ask forgiveness for our own faults but also to appeal to all—to those who have been victimized, to those who have offended, and to all who have felt the wound of this scandal—to be reconciled to God and one another.

Perhaps in a way never before experienced, we feel the power of sin touch our entire Church family in this country; but as St. Paul boldly says, God made Christ "to be sin who did not know sin, so that we might become the righteousness of God in him" (2 Cor 5:21). May we who have known sin experience as well, through a spirit of reconciliation, God's own righteousness. We know that after such profound hurt, healing and reconciliation are beyond human capacity alone. It is God's grace and mercy that will lead us forward, trusting Christ's promise: "for God all things are possible" (Mt 19:26).

In working toward fulfilling this responsibility, we rely, first of all, on Almighty God to sustain us in faith and in the discernment of the right course to take.

We receive fraternal guidance and support from the Holy See that sustains us in this time of trial. In solidarity with Pope Francis, we express heartfelt love and sorrow for the victims of abuse.

We rely on the Catholic faithful of the United States. Nationally and in each diocese/eparchy, the wisdom and expertise of clergy, religious, and laity contribute immensely to confronting the effects of the crisis and taking steps to resolve it. We are filled with gratitude for their great faith, for their generosity, and for the spiritual and moral support that we receive from them.

We acknowledge and re-affirm the faithful service of the vast majority of our priests and deacons and the love that people have for them. They deservedly have our esteem and that of the Catholic people for their good work. It is regrettable that their committed ministerial witness has been overshadowed by this crisis.

In a special way, we acknowledge and thank victims of clergy sexual abuse and their families who have trusted us enough to share their stories and to help us understand more fully the consequences of this reprehensible violation of sacred trust. With Pope Francis, we praise the courage of those who speak out about their abuse; their actions are "a service of love, since for us it sheds light on a terrible darkness in the life of the Church." We pray that "the remnants of the darkness which touch them may be healed" (Address to Victims of Sexual Abuse, July 7, 2014).

Let there now be no doubt or confusion on anyone's part: For us, your bishops, our obligation to protect children and young people and to prevent sexual abuse flows from the mission and example given to us by Jesus Christ himself, in whose name we serve.

As we work to restore trust, we are reminded how Jesus showed constant care for the vulnerable. He inaugurated his ministry with these words of the Prophet Isaiah:

> The Spirit of the Lord is upon me,
> > because he has anointed me
> > > to bring glad tidings to the poor.
>
> He has sent me to proclaim liberty to captives
> > and recovery of sight to the blind,
> > > to let the oppressed go free,
>
> and to proclaim a year acceptable to the Lord. (Lk 4:18-19)

In Matthew 25, the Lord, in his commission to his apostles and disciples, told them that whenever they show mercy and compassion to the least ones, they show it to him.

Jesus extended this care in a tender and urgent way to children, rebuking his disciples for keeping them away from him: "Let the children come to me" (Mt 19:14). And he uttered a grave warning that for anyone who would lead the little ones astray, it would be better for such a person "to have a great millstone hung around his neck and to be drowned in the depths of the sea" (Mt 18:6).

We hear these words of the Lord as prophetic for this moment. With a firm determination to restore the bonds of trust, we bishops recommit ourselves to a continual pastoral outreach to repair the breach with those who have suffered sexual abuse and with all the people of the Church.

In this spirit, over the last sixteen years, the principles and procedures of the *Charter* have been integrated into church life.

- The Secretariat of Child and Youth Protection provides the focus for a consistent, ongoing, and comprehensive approach to creating a safe environment for young people throughout the Church in the United States.

- The Secretariat also provides the means for us to be accountable for achieving the goals of the *Charter*, as demonstrated by its annual reports on the implementation of the *Charter* based on independent compliance audits.

- The National Review Board is carrying on its responsibility to assist in the assessment of diocesan/eparchial compliance with the *Charter for the Protection of Children and Young People*.

- The descriptive study of the nature and scope of sexual abuse of minors by Catholic clergy in the United States, commissioned by the National Review Board, was completed in February 2004. The resulting study, examining the historical period 1950-2002, by the John Jay College of Criminal Justice provides us with a powerful tool not only to examine our past but also to secure our future against such misconduct.

- The U.S. bishops charged the National Review Board to oversee the completion of the *Causes and Context* study. The Study, which calls for ongoing education, situational prevention, and oversight and accountability, was completed in 2011.

- Victims' assistance coordinators are in place throughout our nation to assist dioceses and eparchies in responding to the pastoral needs of the abused.

- Diocesan/eparchial bishops in every diocese/eparchy are advised and greatly assisted by diocesan and eparchial review boards as the bishops make the decisions needed to fulfill the *Charter*.

- Safe environment programs are in place to assist parents and children—and those who work with children—in preventing harm to young people. These programs continually seek to incorporate the most useful developments in the field of child protection.

Through these steps and many others, we remain committed to the safety of our children and young people.

While the number of reported cases of sexual abuse has decreased over the last sixteen years, the harmful effects of this abuse continue to be experienced both by victims and dioceses/eparchies.

Thus it is with a vivid sense of the effort which is still needed to confront the effects of this crisis fully and with the wisdom gained by the experience of the last sixteen years that we have reviewed and revised the *Charter for the Protection of Children and Young People*. We now re-affirm that we will assist in the healing of those who have been injured, will do all in our power to protect children and young people, and will work with our clergy, religious, and laity to restore trust and harmony in our faith communities, as we pray for the Kingdom of God to come, here on earth, as it is in heaven.

To make effective our goals of a safe environment within the Church for children and young people and of preventing sexual abuse of minors by clergy in the future, we, the members of the United States Conference of Catholic Bishops, have outlined in this *Charter* a series of practical and pastoral steps, and we commit ourselves to taking them in our dioceses and eparchies.

✝ TO PROMOTE

Healing and Reconciliation with
Victims/Survivors of Sexual Abuse of Minors

ARTICLE 1. Dioceses/eparchies are to reach out to victims/survivors and their families and demonstrate a sincere commitment to their spiritual and emotional well-being. The first obligation of the Church with regard to the victims is for healing and reconciliation. Each diocese/eparchy is to continue its outreach to every person who has been the victim of sexual abuse as a minor by anyone in church service, whether the abuse was recent or occurred many years in the past. This outreach may include provision of counseling, spiritual assistance, support groups, and other social services agreed upon by the victim and the diocese/eparchy.

Through pastoral outreach to victims and their families, the diocesan/eparchial bishop or his representative is to offer to meet with them, to listen with patience and compassion to their experiences and concerns, and to share the "profound sense of solidarity and concern" expressed by St. John Paul II, in his Address to the Cardinals of the United States and Conference Officers (April 23, 2002). Pope Benedict XVI, too, in his address to the U.S. bishops in 2008 said of the clergy sexual abuse crisis, "It is your God-given responsibility as pastors to bind up the wounds caused by every breach of trust, to foster healing, to promote reconciliation and to reach out with loving concern to those so seriously wronged."

We bishops and eparchs commit ourselves to work as one with our brother priests and deacons to foster reconciliation among all people in our dioceses/eparchies. We especially commit ourselves to work with those individuals who were themselves abused and the communities that have suffered because of the sexual abuse of minors that occurred in their midst.

ARTICLE 2. Dioceses/eparchies are to have policies and procedures in place to respond promptly to any allegation where there is reason to believe that sexual abuse of a minor has occurred. Dioceses/eparchies are to have a competent person or persons to coordinate assistance for the immediate pastoral care of persons who report having been sexually abused as minors by clergy or other church personnel. The procedures for those making a complaint are to be readily available in printed form and other media in the principal languages in which the liturgy is celebrated in the diocese/eparchy and be the subject of public announcements at least annually.

Dioceses/eparchies are also to have a review board that functions as a confidential consultative body to the bishop/eparch. The majority of its members are to be lay persons not in the employ of the diocese/eparchy (see Norm 5 in *Essential Norms for Diocesan/Eparchial Policies Dealing with Allegations of Sexual Abuse of Minors by Priests or Deacons*, 2006). This board is to advise the diocesan/eparchial bishop in his assessment of allegations of sexual abuse of minors and in his determination of a cleric's suitability for ministry. It is regularly to review diocesan/eparchial policies and procedures for dealing with sexual abuse of minors. Also, the board can review these matters both retrospectively and prospectively and give advice on all aspects of responses in connection with these cases.

ARTICLE 3. Dioceses/eparchies are not to enter into settlements which bind the parties to confidentiality, unless the victim/survivor requests confidentiality and this request is noted in the text of the agreement.

✝
TO GUARANTEE
an Effective Response to Allegations of
Sexual Abuse of Minors

ARTICLE 4. Dioceses/eparchies are to report an allegation of sexual abuse of a person who is a minor to the public authorities with due regard for the seal of the Sacrament of Penance. Diocesan/eparchial personnel are to comply with all applicable civil laws with respect to the reporting of allegations of sexual abuse of minors to civil authorities and cooperate in their investigation in accord with the law of the jurisdiction in question.

Dioceses/eparchies are to cooperate with public authorities about reporting cases even when the person is no longer a minor.

In every instance, dioceses/eparchies are to advise victims of their right to make a report to public authorities and support this right.

ARTICLE 5. We affirm the words of St. John Paul II, in his Address to the Cardinals of the United States and Conference Officers: "There is no place in the priesthood or religious life for those who would harm the young." Pope Francis has consistently reiterated this with victims of clergy sexual abuse.

Sexual abuse of a minor by a cleric is a crime in the universal law of the Church (CIC, c. 1395 §2; CCEO, c. 1453 §1). Because of the seriousness of this matter, jurisdiction has been reserved to the Congregation for the Doctrine of the Faith (*Motu proprio Sacramentorum sanctitatis tutela*, AAS 93, 2001). Sexual abuse of a minor is also a crime in all civil jurisdictions in the United States.

Diocesan/eparchial policy is to provide that for even a single act of sexual abuse of a minor—whenever it occurred—which is admitted or established after an appropriate process in accord with canon law, the offending priest or deacon is to be permanently removed from ministry and, if warranted, dismissed from the clerical state. In keeping with the stated purpose of this *Charter*, an offending priest or deacon is to be offered therapeutic professional assistance both for the purpose of prevention and also for his own healing and well-being.

The diocesan/eparchial bishop is to exercise his power of governance, within the parameters of the universal law of the Church, to ensure that any priest or deacon subject to his governance who has committed even one act of sexual abuse of a minor as described below (see notes) shall not continue in ministry.

A priest or deacon who is accused of sexual abuse of a minor is to be accorded the presumption of innocence during the investigation of the allegation and all appropriate steps are to be taken to protect his reputation. He is to be encouraged to retain the assistance of civil and canonical counsel. If the allegation is deemed not substantiated, every step possible is to be taken to restore his good name, should it have been harmed.

In fulfilling this article, dioceses/eparchies are to follow the requirements of the universal law of the Church and of the *Essential Norms* approved for the United States.

ARTICLE 6. There are to be clear and well publicized diocesan/eparchial standards of ministerial behavior and appropriate boundaries for clergy and for any other paid personnel and volunteers of the Church with regard to their contact with minors.

ARTICLE 7. Dioceses/eparchies are to be open and transparent in communicating with the public about sexual abuse of minors by clergy within the confines of respect for the privacy and the reputation of the individuals involved. This is especially so with regard to informing parish and other church communities directly affected by sexual abuse of a minor.

✝ TO ENSURE

the Accountability of Our Procedures

ARTICLE 8. The Committee on the Protection of Children and Young People is a standing committee of the United States Conference of Catholic Bishops. Its membership is to include representation from all the episcopal regions of the country, with new appointments staggered to maintain continuity in the effort to protect children and youth.

The Committee is to advise the USCCB on all matters related to child and youth protection and is to oversee the development of the plans, programs, and budget of the Secretariat of Child and Youth Protection. It is to provide the USCCB with comprehensive planning and recommendations concerning child and youth protection by coordinating the efforts of the Secretariat and the National Review Board.

ARTICLE 9. The Secretariat of Child and Youth Protection, established by the Conference of Catholic Bishops, is to staff the Committee on the Protection of Children and Young People and be a resource for dioceses/eparchies for the implementation of "safe environment" programs and for suggested training and development of diocesan personnel responsible for child and youth protection programs, taking into account the financial and other resources, as well as the population, area, and demographics of the diocese/eparchy.

The Secretariat is to produce an annual public report on the progress made in implementing and maintaining the standards in this *Charter*. The report is to be based on an annual audit process whose method, scope, and cost are to be approved by the Administrative Committee on the recommendation of the Committee on the Protection of Children and Young People. This public report is to include the names of those dioceses/eparchies which the audit shows are not in compliance with the provisions and expectations of the *Charter*. The audit method refers to the process and techniques used to determine compliance with the *Charter*. The audit scope relates to the focus, parameters, and time period for the matters to be examined during an individual audit.

As a member of the Conference staff, the Executive Director of the Secretariat is appointed by and reports to the General Secretary. The Executive Director is to provide the Committee on the Protection of Children and Young People and the National Review Board with regular reports of the Secretariat's activities.

ARTICLE 10. The whole Church, at both the diocesan/eparchial and national levels, must be engaged in maintaining safe environments in the Church for children and young people.

The Committee on the Protection of Children and Young People is to be assisted by the National Review Board, a consultative body established in 2002 by the USCCB. The Board will review the annual report of the Secretariat of Child and Youth Protection on the implementation of this *Charter* in each diocese/eparchy and any recommendations that emerge from it, and offer its own assessment regarding its approval and publication to the Conference President.

The Board will also advise the Conference President on future members. The Board members are appointed by the Conference President in consultation with the Administrative Committee and are accountable to him and to the USCCB Executive Committee. Before a candidate is contacted, the Conference President is to seek and obtain, in writing, the endorsement of the candidate's diocesan bishop. The Board is to operate in accord with the statutes and bylaws of the USCCB and within procedural guidelines developed by the Board in consultation with the Committee on the Protection of Children and Young People and approved by the USCCB Administrative Committee. These guidelines set forth such matters as the Board's purpose and responsibility, officers, terms of office, and frequency of reports to the Conference President on its activities.

The Board will offer its advice as it collaborates with the Committee on the Protection of Children and Young People on matters of child and youth protection, specifically on policies and best practices. For example, the Board will continue to monitor the recommendations derived from the *Causes and Context* study. The Board and Committee on the Protection of Children and Young People will meet jointly every year.

The Board will review the work of the Secretariat of Child and Youth Protection and make recommendations to the Executive Director. It will assist the Executive Director in the development of resources for dioceses.

ARTICLE 11. The President of the Conference is to inform the Holy See of this revised *Charter* to indicate the manner in which we, the Catholic bishops, together with the entire Church in the United States, intend to continue our commitment to the protection of children and young people. The President is also to share with the Holy See the annual reports on the implementation of the *Charter*.

✝ TO PROTECT
the Faithful in the Future

ARTICLE 12. Dioceses/eparchies are to maintain "safe environment" programs which the diocesan/eparchial bishop deems to be in accord with Catholic moral principles. They are to be conducted cooperatively with parents, civil authorities, educators, and community organizations to provide education and training for minors, parents, ministers, employees, volunteers, and others about ways to sustain and foster a safe environment for minors. Dioceses/eparchies are to make clear to clergy and all members of the community the standards of conduct for clergy and other persons with regard to their contact with minors.

ARTICLE 13. The diocesan/eparchial bishop is to evaluate the background of all incardinated priests and deacons. When a priest or deacon, not incardinated in the diocese/eparchy, is to engage in ministry in the diocese/eparchy, regardless of the length of time, the evaluation of his background may be satisfied through a written attestation of suitability for ministry supplied by his proper ordinary/major superior to the diocese/eparchy. Dioceses/eparchies are to evaluate the background of all their respective diocesan/eparchial and parish/school or other paid personnel and volunteers whose duties include contact with minors. Specifically, they are to utilize the resources of law enforcement and other community agencies. Each diocese/eparchy is to determine the application/renewal of background checks according to local practice. In addition, they are to employ adequate screening and evaluative techniques in deciding the fitness of candidates for ordination (see USCCB, *Program of Priestly Formation* [Fifth Edition], 2006, no. 39 and the *National Directory for the Formation, Ministry and Life of Permanent Deacons in the United States*, n.178 j).[2]

ARTICLE 14. Transfers of all priests and deacons who have committed an act of sexual abuse against a minor for residence, including retirement, shall be in accord with Norm 12 of the Essential Norms (see *Proposed Guidelines on the Transfer or Assignment of Clergy and Religious*, adopted by the USCCB, the Conference of Major Superiors of Men [CMSM], the Leadership Conference of Women Religious [LCWR], and the Council of Major Superiors of Women Religious [CMSWR] in 1993).

ARTICLE 15. To ensure continuing collaboration and mutuality of effort in the protection of children and young people on the part of the bishops and religious ordinaries, two representatives of the Conference of Major Superiors of Men are to serve as consultants to the Committee on the Protection of Children and Young People. At the invitation of the Major Superiors, the Committee will designate two of its members to consult with its counterpart at CMSM. Diocesan/eparchial bishops and major superiors of clerical institutes or their delegates are to meet periodically to coordinate their roles concerning the issue of allegations made against a cleric member of a religious institute ministering in a diocese/eparchy.

ARTICLE 16. Given the extent of the problem of the sexual abuse of minors in our society, we are willing to cooperate with other churches and ecclesial communities, other religious bodies, institutions of learning, and other interested organizations in conducting research in this area.

ARTICLE 17. We commit ourselves to work individually in our dioceses/eparchies and together as a Conference, through the appropriate committees, to strengthen our programs both for initial priestly and diaconal formation and their ongoing formation. With renewed urgency, we will promote programs of human formation for chastity and celibacy for both seminarians and priests based upon the criteria found in *Pastores dabo vobis, no. 50*, the *Program of Priestly Formation*, and the *Basic Plan for the Ongoing Formation of Priests*, as well as similar, appropriate programs for deacons based upon the criteria found in the *National Directory for the Formation, Ministry and Life of Permanent Deacons in the United States*. We will continue to assist priests, deacons, and seminarians in living out their vocation in faithful and integral ways.

✝
CONCLUSION

As we wrote in 2002, "It is within this context of the essential soundness of the priesthood and of the deep faith of our brothers and sisters in the Church that we know that we can meet and resolve this crisis for now and the future."

We reaffirm that the vast majority of priests and deacons serve their people faithfully and that they have their esteem and affection. They also have our respect and support and our commitment to their good names and well-being.

An essential means of dealing with the crisis is prayer for healing and reconciliation, and acts of reparation for the grave offense to God and the deep wound inflicted upon his holy people. Closely connected to prayer and acts of reparation is the call to holiness of life and the care of the diocesan/eparchial bishop to ensure that he and his priests and deacons avail themselves of the proven ways of avoiding sin and growing in holiness of life.

It is with reliance on the grace of God and in a spirit of prayer and penance that we renew the pledges which we made in the 2002 *Charter*:

> **We pledge most solemnly to one another and to you, God's people, that we will work to our utmost for the protection of children and youth.**
>
> **We pledge that we will devote to this goal the resources and personnel necessary to accomplish it.**

We pledge that we will do our best to ordain to the diaconate and priesthood and put into positions of trust only those who share this commitment to protecting children and youth.

We pledge that we will work toward healing and reconciliation for those sexually abused by clerics.

Much has been done to honor these pledges. We devoutly pray that God who has begun this good work in us will bring it to fulfillment.

This *Charter* is published for the dioceses/eparchies of the United States. It is to be reviewed again after seven years by the Committee on the Protection of Children and Young People with the advice of the National Review Board. The results of this review are to be presented to the full Conference of Bishops for confirmation. Authoritative interpretations of its provisions are reserved to the Conference of Bishops.

NOTES

1   For purposes of this *Charter*, the offense of sexual abuse of a minor will be understood in accord with the provisions of *Sacramentorum sanctitatis tutela* (SST), article 6, which reads:

   §1. The more grave delicts against morals which are reserved to the Congregation for the Doctrine of the Faith are:
   1° the delict against the sixth commandment of the Decalogue committed by a cleric with a minor below the age of eighteen years; in this case, a person who habitually lacks the use of reason is to be considered equivalent to a minor.
   2° the acquisition, possession, or distribution by a cleric of pornographic images of minors under the age of fourteen, for purposes of sexual gratification, by whatever means or using whatever technology;

   §2. A cleric who commits the delicts mentioned above in §1 is to be punished according to the gravity of his crime, not excluding dismissal or deposition.

In view of the Circular Letter from the Congregation for the Doctrine of the Faith, dated May 3, 2011, which calls for "mak[ing] allowance for the legislation of the country where the Conference is located," Section III(g), we will apply the federal legal age for defining child pornography, which includes pornographic images of minors under the age of eighteen, for assessing a cleric's suitability for ministry and for complying with civil reporting statutes.

If there is any doubt whether a specific act qualifies as an external, objectively grave violation, the writings of recognized moral theologians should be consulted, and the opinions of recognized experts should be appropriately obtained (*Canonical Delicts Involving Sexual Misconduct and Dismissal from the Clerical State*, 1995, p. 6). Ultimately, it is the responsibility of the diocesan bishop/eparch, with the advice of a qualified review board, to determine the gravity of the alleged act.

2 In 2009, after consultation with members of the USCCB Committee on the Protection of Children and Young People and the Conference of Major Superiors of Men and approval from the USCCB Committee on Canonical Affairs and Church Governance, additional Model Letters of Suitability, now available on the USCCB website, were agreed upon and published for use by bishops and major superiors in situations which involve both temporary and extended ministry for clerics.

Essential Norms for Diocesan/Eparchial Policies Dealing with Allegations of Sexual Abuse of Minors by Priests or Deacons

Office of the President
3211 FOURTH STREET NE • WASHINGTON DC 20017-1194
202-541-3100 • FAX 202-541-3166

Most Reverend William S. Skylstad, D.D.
Bishop of Spokane

May 5, 2006

THE UNITED STATES CONFERENCE OF CATHOLIC BISHOPS

DECREE OF PROMULGATION

On November 13, 2002, the members of the United States Conference of Catholic Bishops approved as particular law the *Essential Norms for Diocesan/Eparchial Policies Dealing with Allegations of Sexual Abuse of Minors by Priests or Deacons*. Following the grant of the required *recognitio* by the Congregation for Bishops on December 8, 2002, the *Essential Norms* were promulgated by the President of the same Conference on December 12, 2002.

Thereafter, on June 17, 2005, the members of the United States Conference of Catholic Bishops approved a revised text of the *Essential Norms*. By a decree dated January 1, 2006, and signed by His Eminence, Giovanni Battista Cardinal Re, Prefect of the Congregation for Bishops, and His Excellency, the Most Reverend Francesco Monterisi, Secretary of the same Congregation, the *recognitio* originally granted to the *Essential Norms* of 2002 was extended to the revised version *donec aliter provideatur*.

As President of the United States Conference of Catholic Bishops, I therefore decree the promulgation of the *Essential Norms* of June 17, 2005. These *Norms* shall obtain force on May 15, 2006, and so shall from that day bind as particular law all Dioceses and Eparchies of the United States Conference of Catholic Bishops.

Most Reverend William S. Skylstad
Bishop of Spokane
President, USCCB

Reverend Monsignor David J. Malloy
General Secretary

✝
PREAMBLE

On June 14, 2002, the United States Conference of Catholic Bishops approved a *Charter for the Protection of Children and Young People*. The charter addresses the Church's commitment to deal appropriately and effectively with cases of sexual abuse of minors by priests, deacons, and other church personnel (i.e., employees and volunteers). The bishops of the United States have promised to reach out to those who have been sexually abused as minors by anyone serving the Church in ministry, employment, or a volunteer position, whether the sexual abuse was recent or occurred many years ago. They stated that they would be as open as possible with the people in parishes and communities about instances of sexual abuse of minors, with respect always for the privacy and the reputation of the individuals involved. They have committed themselves to the pastoral and spiritual care and emotional well-being of those who have been sexually abused and of their families.

In addition, the bishops will work with parents, civil authorities, educators, and various organizations in the community to make and maintain the safest environment for minors. In the same way, the bishops have pledged to evaluate the background of seminary applicants as well as all church personnel who have responsibility for the care and supervision of children and young people.

Therefore, to ensure that each diocese/eparchy in the United States of America will have procedures in place to respond promptly to all allegations of sexual abuse of minors, the United States Conference of Catholic Bishops decrees these norms for diocesan/eparchial policies dealing with allegations of sexual abuse of minors by diocesan and religious priests or deacons.[1] These norms are complementary to the universal law of the Church and are to be interpreted in accordance with that law. The Church has traditionally considered the sexual abuse of minors a grave delict and punishes the offender with penalties, not excluding dismissal from the clerical state if the case so warrants.

For purposes of these Norms, sexual abuse shall include any offense by a cleric against the Sixth Commandment of the Decalogue with a minor as understood in CIC, canon 1395 §2, and CCEO, canon 1453 §1 (*Sacramentorum sanctitatis tutela*, article 6 §1).[2]

✝ NORMS

1. These Essential Norms have been granted *recognitio* by the Holy See. Having been legitimately promulgated in accordance with the practice of the United States Conference of Catholic Bishops on May 5, 2006, they constitute particular law for all the dioceses/eparchies of the United States of America.[3]

2. Each diocese/eparchy will have a written policy on the sexual abuse of minors by priests and deacons, as well as by other church personnel. This policy is to comply fully with, and is to specify in more detail, the steps to be taken in implementing the requirements of canon law, particularly CIC, canons 1717-1719, and CCEO, canons 1468-1470. A copy of this policy will be filed with the United States Conference of Catholic Bishops within three months of the effective date of these norms. Copies of any eventual revisions of the written diocesan/eparchial policy are also to be filed with the United States Conference of Catholic Bishops within three months of such modifications.

3. Each diocese/eparchy will designate a competent person to coordinate assistance for the immediate pastoral care of persons who claim to have been sexually abused when they were minors by priests or deacons.

4. To assist diocesan/eparchial bishops, each diocese/eparchy will also have a review board which will function as a confidential consultative

body to the bishop/eparch in discharging his responsibilities. The functions of this board may include

   a. advising the diocesan bishop/eparch in his assessment of allegations of sexual abuse of minors and in his determination of suitability for ministry;
   b. reviewing diocesan/eparchial policies for dealing with sexual abuse of minors; and
   c. offering advice on all aspects of these cases, whether retrospectively or prospectively.

5. The review board, established by the diocesan/eparchial bishop, will be composed of at least five persons of outstanding integrity and good judgment in full communion with the Church. The majority of the review board members will be lay persons who are not in the employ of the diocese/eparchy; but at least one member should be a priest who is an experienced and respected pastor of the diocese/eparchy in question, and at least one member should have particular expertise in the treatment of the sexual abuse of minors. The members will be appointed for a term of five years, which can be renewed. It is desirable that the Promoter of Justice participate in the meetings of the review board.

6. When an allegation of sexual abuse of a minor by a priest or deacon is received, a preliminary investigation in accordance with canon law will be initiated and conducted promptly and objectively (CIC, c. 1717; CCEO, c. 1468). During the investigation the accused enjoys the presumption of innocence, and all appropriate steps shall be taken to protect his reputation. The accused will be encouraged to retain the assistance of civil and canonical counsel and will be promptly notified of the results of the investigation. When there is sufficient evidence that sexual abuse of a minor has occurred, the Congregation of the Doctrine of the Faith shall be notified. The bishop/eparch shall then apply the precautionary measures mentioned in CIC, canon 1722, or CCEO, canon 1473—i.e., withdraw the accused from exercising the sacred ministry or any ecclesiastical office or function, impose or prohibit residence in a given place or territory, and prohibit public participation in the Most Holy Eucharist pending the outcome of the process.[4]

7. The alleged offender may be requested to seek, and may be urged voluntarily to comply with, an appropriate medical and psychological evaluation at a facility mutually acceptable to the diocese/eparchy and to the accused.

8. When even a single act of sexual abuse by a priest or deacon is admitted or is established after an appropriate process in accord with canon law, the offending priest or deacon will be removed permanently from ecclesiastical ministry, not excluding dismissal from the clerical state, if the case so warrants (SST, Art. 6; CIC, c. 1395 §2; CCEO, c. 1453 §1).[5]

> **a.** In every case involving canonical penalties, the processes provided for in canon law must be observed, and the various provisions of canon law must be considered (cf. *Canonical Delicts Involving Sexual Misconduct and Dismissal from the Clerical State*, 1995; Letter from the Congregation for the Doctrine of the Faith, May 18, 2001). Unless the Congregation for the Doctrine of the Faith, having been notified, calls the case to itself because of special circumstances, it will direct the diocesan bishop/eparch to proceed (Article 13, "Procedural Norms" for *Motu proprio Sacramentorum sanctitatis tutela*, AAS, 93, 2001, p. 787). If the case would otherwise be barred by prescription, because sexual abuse of a minor is a grave offense, the bishop/eparch may apply to the Congregation for the Doctrine of the Faith

for a derogation from the prescription, while indicating relevant grave reasons. For the sake of canonical due process, the accused is to be encouraged to retain the assistance of civil and canonical counsel. When necessary, the diocese/eparchy will supply canonical counsel to a priest. The provisions of CIC, canon 1722, or CCEO, canon 1473, shall be implemented during the pendency of the penal process.

    b.   If the penalty of dismissal from the clerical state has not been applied (e.g., for reasons of advanced age or infirmity), the offender ought to lead a life of prayer and penance. He will not be permitted to celebrate Mass publicly or to administer the sacraments. He is to be instructed not to wear clerical garb, or to present himself publicly as a priest.

9. At all times, the diocesan bishop/eparch has the executive power of governance, within the parameters of the universal law of the Church, through an administrative act, to remove an offending cleric from office, to remove or restrict his faculties, and to limit his exercise of priestly ministry.[6] Because sexual abuse of a minor by a cleric is a crime in the universal law of the Church (CIC, c. 1395 §2; CCEO, c. 1453 §1) and is a crime in all civil jurisdictions in the United States, for the sake of the common good and observing the provisions of canon law, the diocesan bishop/eparch shall exercise this power of governance to ensure that any priest or deacon who has committed even one act of sexual abuse of a minor as described above shall not continue in active ministry.[7]

10. The priest or deacon may at any time request a dispensation from the obligations of the clerical state. In exceptional cases, the bishop/eparch may request of the Holy Father the dismissal of the priest or deacon from the clerical state *ex officio*, even without the consent of the priest or deacon.

11. The diocese/eparchy will comply with all applicable civil laws with respect to the reporting of allegations of sexual abuse of minors to civil authorities and will cooperate in their investigation. In every instance, the diocese/eparchy will advise and support a person's right to make a report to public authorities.[8]

12. No priest or deacon who has committed an act of sexual abuse of a minor may be transferred for a ministerial assignment in another diocese/eparchy. Every bishop/eparch who receives a priest or deacon from outside his jurisdiction will obtain the necessary information regarding any past act of sexual abuse of a minor by the priest or deacon in question.

Before such a diocesan/eparchial priest or deacon can be transferred for residence to another diocese/eparchy, his diocesan/eparchial bishop shall forward, in a confidential manner, to the bishop of the proposed place of residence any and all information concerning any act of sexual abuse of a minor and any other information indicating that he has been or may be a danger to children or young people.

In the case of the assignment for residence of such a clerical member of an institute or a society into a local community within a diocese/eparchy, the major superior shall inform the diocesan/eparchial bishop and share with him in a manner respecting the limitations of confidentiality found in canon and civil law all information concerning any act of sexual abuse of a minor and any other information indicating that he has been or may be a danger to children or young people so that the bishop/eparch can make an informed judgment that suitable safeguards are in place for the protection of children and young people. This will be done with due recognition of the legitimate authority of the bishop/eparch; of the provisions of CIC, canon 678 (CCEO, canons 415 §1 and 554 §2), and of CIC, canon 679; and of the autonomy of the religious life (CIC, c. 586).

13. Care will always be taken to protect the rights of all parties involved, particularly those of the person claiming to have been sexually abused and of the person against whom the charge has been made. When an accusation has been shown to be unfounded, every step possible will be taken to restore the good name of the person falsely accused.

NOTES
1. These Norms constitute particular law for the dioceses, eparchies, clerical religious institutes, and societies of apostolic life of the United States with respect to all priests and deacons in the ecclesiastical ministry of the Church in the United States. When a major superior of a clerical religious institute or society of apostolic life applies and interprets them for the internal life and governance of the institute or society, he has the obligation to do so according to the universal law of the Church and the proper law of the institute or society.
2. If there is any doubt whether a specific act qualifies as an external, objectively grave violation, the writings of recognized moral theologians should be consulted, and the opinions of recognized experts should be appropriately obtained (*Canonical Delicts*, p. 6). Ultimately, it is the responsibility of the diocesan bishop/eparch, with the advice of a qualified review board, to determine the gravity of the alleged act.
3. Due regard must be given to the proper legislative authority of each Eastern Catholic Church.
4. Article 19 *Sacramentum sanctitatis tutela* states, "With due regard for the right of the Ordinary to impose from the outset of the preliminary investigation those measures which are established in can. 1722 of the Code of Canon Law, or in can. 1473 of the Code of Canons of the Eastern Churches, the respective presiding judge may, at the request of the Promoter of Justice, exercise the same power under the same conditions determined in the canons themselves."
5. Removal from ministry is required whether or not the cleric is diagnosed by qualified experts as a pedophile or as suffering from a related sexual disorder that requires professional treatment. With regard to the use of the phrase "ecclesiastical ministry," by clerical members of institutes of consecrated life and societies of apostolic life, the provisions of canons 678 and 738 also apply, with due regard for canons 586 and 732.
6. Cf. CIC, cc. 35-58, 149, 157, 187-189, 192-195, 277 §3, 381 §1, 383, 391, 1348, and 1740-1747. Cf. also CCEO, cc. 1510 §1 and 2, 1°-2°, 1511, 1512

§§1-2, 1513 §§2-3 and 5, 1514-1516, 1517 §1, 1518, 1519 §2, 1520 §§1-3, 1521, 1522 §1, 1523-1526, 940, 946, 967-971, 974-977, 374, 178, 192 §§1-3, 193 §2, 191, and 1389-1396.

7   The diocesan bishop/eparch may exercise his executive power of governance to take one or more of the following administrative actions (CIC, cc. 381, 129ff.; CCEO, cc. 178, 979ff.):

   a. He may request that the accused freely resign from any currently held ecclesiastical office (CIC, cc. 187-189; CCEO, cc. 967-971).
   b. Should the accused decline to resign and should the diocesan bishop/eparch judge the accused to be truly not suitable (CIC, c. 149 §1; CCEO, c. 940) at this time for holding an office previously freely conferred (CIC, c. 157), then he may remove that person from office observing the required canonical procedures (CIC, cc. 192-195, 1740-1747; CCEO, cc. 974-977, 1389-1396).
   c. For a cleric who holds no office in the diocese/eparchy, any previously delegated faculties may be administratively removed (CIC, cc. 391 §1 and 142 §1; CCEO, cc. 191 §1 and 992 §1), while any *de iure* faculties may be removed or restricted by the competent authority as provided in law (e.g., CIC, c. 764; CCEO, c. 610 §§2-3).
   d. The diocesan bishop/eparch may also determine that circumstances surrounding a particular case constitute the just and reasonable cause for a priest to celebrate the Eucharist with no member of the faithful present (CIC, c. 906). The bishop may forbid the priest to celebrate the Eucharist publicly and to administer the sacraments, for the good of the Church and for his own good.
   e. Depending on the gravity of the case, the diocesan bishop/eparch may also dispense (CIC, cc. 85-88; CCEO, cc. 1536 §1–1538) the cleric from the obligation of wearing clerical attire (CIC, c. 284; CCEO, c. 387) and may urge that he not do so, for the good of the Church and for his own good.

   These administrative actions shall be taken in writing and by means of decrees (CIC, cc. 47-58; CCEO, cc. 1510 §2, 1°-2°, 1511, 1513 §§2-3 and 5, 1514, 1517 §1, 1518, 1519 §2, 1520) so that the cleric affected is afforded the opportunity of recourse against them in accord with canon law (CIC, cc. 1734ff.; CCEO, cc. 999ff.).

8   The necessary observance of the canonical norms internal to the Church is not intended in any way to hinder the course of any civil action that may be operative. At the same time, the Church reaffirms her right to enact legislation binding on all her members concerning the ecclesiastical dimensions of the delict of sexual abuse of minors.

A Statement of Episcopal Commitment

✝
A STATEMENT
of Episcopal Commitment

We bishops pledge again to respond to the demands of the *Charter* in a way that manifests our accountability to God, to God's people, and to one another. Individually and together, we acknowledge mistakes in the past when some bishops transferred, from one assignment to another, priests who abused minors. We recognize our roles in the suffering this has caused, and we continue to ask forgiveness for it.

Without at all diminishing the importance of broader accountability, this statement focuses on the accountability which flows from our episcopal communion and fraternal solidarity, a moral responsibility we have with and for each other.

While bishops are ordained primarily for their diocese or eparchy, we are called as well to protect the unity and to promote the common discipline of the whole Church (CIC, c. 392; CCEO, c. 201). Participating in the college of bishops, each bishop is responsible to act in a manner that reflects both effective and affective collegiality.

Respecting the legitimate rights of bishops who are directly accountable to the Holy See, in a spirit of collegiality and fraternity we renew our commitment to the following:

1. Within each of our provinces, we will assist each other to interpret correctly and implement, within our respective jurisdictions, the *Charter for the Protection of Children and Young People*, always respecting Church law and striving to reflect the Gospel.

2. We will apply the requirements of the *Charter* also to ourselves, respecting always Church law as it applies to bishops. Therefore, if a bishop is accused of the sexual abuse of a minor, the accused bishop is obliged to inform the Apostolic Nuncio. If another bishop becomes aware of the sexual abuse of a minor by another bishop or of an allegation of the sexual abuse of a minor by a bishop, he too is obliged to inform the Apostolic Nuncio and comply with applicable civil laws.

3. In cases of financial demands for settlements involving allegations of any sexual misconduct by a bishop, he, or any of us who become aware of it, is obliged to inform the Apostolic Nuncio.

4. Within each of our provinces, as an expression of collegiality, including fraternal support, fraternal challenge and fraternal correction, we will engage in ongoing mutual reflection upon our commitment to holiness of life and upon the exercise of our episcopal ministry.

In making this statement, we firmly uphold the dignity of every human being and renew our commitment to live and promote the chastity required of all followers of Christ and especially of deacons, priests and bishops.

This Statement of Episcopal Commitment will be reviewed by the Committee on Clergy, Consecrated Life and Vocations upon the next review of the *Charter*.